Grandma's Food Proce

Natural Health Series

Dueep J. Singh

Mendon Cottage Books

JD-Biz Publishing

Disclaimer

The information is this book is provided for informational purposes only. It is not intended to be used and medical advice or a substitute for proper medical treatment by a qualified health care provider. The information is believed to be accurate as presented based on research by the author.

The contents have not been evaluated by the U.S. Food and Drug Administration or any other Government or Health Organization and the contents in this book are not to be used to treat cure or prevent disease.

The author or publisher is not responsible for the use or safety of any diet, procedure or treatment mentioned in this book. The author or publisher is not responsible for errors or omissions that may exist.

Warning

The Book is for informational purposes only and before taking on any diet, treatment or medical procedure, it is recommended to consult with your primary health care provider.

Check out more grandma series books here on Amazon.

Grandma's Books on Amazon

Check out some of the other Healthy Gardening Series books at Amazon.com

Gardening Series on Amazon

Check out some of the other Health Learning Series books at Amazon.com

Health Learning Series on Amazon

Series books at Amazon.com

Health Learning Series on Amazon

Table of Contents

Introduction

Ever since mankind has been inventing new food making processes like boiling, baking, brewing, stewing, the science of food preparation down the ages has not changed much, even though the world has gone through astonishing technological development.

However, many of these food making, and preparing processes have been made easier, with the use of technical machinery. So in grandmother's time, when food was prepared by chopping, slicing, dicing, and mixing and mincing was done by beating up the spices and the herbs in a pestle and mortar, nowadays we have food processors ready at hand.

This book introduces you to a brand-new kitchen revolution and Renaissance – the using of a food processor to prepare food easily. In many of the recipes given below, you may not need to cook anything or cook things to a minimum. All you have to do is put the ingredients in the food processor, mix, blend, pulverize, make into a paste and serve.

Thanks to the amazing high quality food processor brands available to you in the market today, not only experienced cooks, but novices also are getting more adventurous in the matters of different cuisines from all the corners of the globe.

Also, with the help of a food processor, a treasured family recipe can be perfected.

There was a time when grandma made it by whipping cream by hand or getting one of the grandchildren to do all the cutting, chopping, mixing and other hard labor and kitchen drudgery work.

But today, thanks to food processors, exotic spices and unusual vegetables and fruits can appear on more and more tables as the spirit of culinary adventure allows you to experiment and discover new tastes, textures and delicacies.

Naturally, and adventurous cook is also looking for shorter and more efficient ways to make her and his culinary discoveries. We definitely do not have the time or the inclination to spend hours in the kitchen chopping, grinding, mixing and blending in a sweltering kitchen. Grandma may have enjoyed slaving for hours over a hot kitchen stove, but she had absolutely no other option. The family had to be fed.

Luckily, we do not have to undergo that sort of trouble every day, when we have time-saving kitchen techniques and equipment ready at hand. Out of these multipurpose food processors open up a brand new world of different cooking possibilities.

These machines should normally do the work of a skilled care of hands, wielding a finely honed chef's knife, Cleaver or whisk. Besides this, so much energy and effort is saved.

For example, if grandma made mayonnaise, she sat herself down on a chair with an egg whisk and bowl. Then she kept beating the eggs until they were fluffy. After that, she added oil and vinegar, drop by drop until the mayonnaise got emulsified. It took anywhere between 20 to 30 minutes for her to prepare a long-lasting mayonnaise. But today, grandma's granddaughter can whisk mayonnaise in her handy food processor in anywhere between one – 2 minutes and get delicious, thick and nutritious mayonnaise.

So this is one piece of good kitchen equipment, which is going to liberate the dormant gourmet in you, as well as motivate the everyday cook to try revolutionary new cooking techniques made possible with a multipurpose food processor machine.

So thanks to your handy food processor, you can try anything now from traditional and exotic salad dressings, subtly flavored and savory soups, hearty and full meal dishes, supporting vegetable dishes and delicious desserts.

Types of Multipurpose Food Processors

Ever since multiple food processors came into existence in the beginning of the 20th-century, the basic types have remained the same. You can find the freestanding multipurpose machine that has a power base and various attachments – blenders, grinders, slices, shredders, and other accessories. On the other hand, you may find blenders where blending, slicing and shredding and other tasks can be done very easily just by changing a blade.

Many of the popular food processors available in the market today include Kenwood, Braun, Cuisinart , Moulinex etc.. So before you buy a multipurpose food processor, you would want to look at your budget and the uses to which you are going to put it. If you are buying a machine which just adorns the corner of your kitchen slab and is used once a month, you can manage with one of the lesser-known brands. But if you want to put your machine to heavy use every day, I would suggest considering the money spent in buying a good machine to be an investment.

Many of these food processors are rather expensive and beyond our budget. But good brand names are an once-in-a-lifetime buy.[1]

---

[1] But even these machines may let you down, as it happened for dad. He bought a multipurpose Mini Moulinex –a French company – in Germany in the early 70s and brought it back home. Only to find out that it did not work. Naturally, he could not send it back all the way to Düsseldorf for repairs. So he had to open it and use his engineering skills. It had a wire/connection loose. He repaired it and that machine worked for the next 10 years, chopping, grinding, mixing, blending and serving all the kitchen functions for the family.

But if he had stayed on in Germany, he would have thrown it out, told all his friends not to buy a Moulinex ever and bought a more reliable Braun instead. So test drive your machine, and get your guaranty card. Best of all, do not buy electronics abroad because they may not work when you come back home and all that money/customs duty you paid on it is that much waste.

How to Work with a Multipurpose Food Processor

Remember to put the lid on.

If you have just entered the brand-new world of cuisine, learning how to cook, your first step should be how to get acquainted with the food processor. Practice makes perfect and experience is going to make you starting to use your processor often and instinctively.

There will soon come a time when instead of reaching for your cleaver and sharp set of kitchen knives, you are just going to toss the ingredients in your food processor and give it a whirl.

Remember to study all the instructions that come with the machine and keep the general instructions in mind when working with the recipes given below in this book.

Certain machines have some restrictions on what they can and cannot do, depending on their functions and accessories. So know the limitations of your machine.

For all those who have become so used to doing all the kitchen tasks laboriously by hand, because we were trained that way, this is the habit that is going to be hard to break, but once one has made the adjustment, you will find it hard to return to slicing, chopping, grinding and mixing by hand.

So it does not matter whether you are cooking for your family or for an elegant dinner party; plenty of time and energy can be saved by using your food processor efficiently.

The results are always impressive! You do not need to have to be trained at a fancy cooking school to whip up a pizza for your kids, or a mousse with a melt – in – the – mouth velvet smooth texture. Also, you do not have to apprentice yourself to Master Liu, your city's Oriental master chef teacher in order to learn how to thinly slice, dice, chop and cut vegetables in the twinkling of an eye.

All this and more is going to be done with the help of your reliable Food Processor.

Appetizers

Appetizers are those savories, which just whet your appetite for more delicious food to come. These are going to include cheeses, pate , dips, wafers, pastries, snacks and other finger food, which is served before the main course.

We are starting our appetizers with a delicious layer of savory chicken liver pate on the bottom and a layer of cream cheese flavored with Madeira on the top. You can either make the garnish as elaborate or as simple as you wish by using green capsicum and read tomatoes for flowers and thin slices of green pepper for stems. This is called

Pâté de foie a la Crème

This pâté has been wrapped up in leaves, and is topped with caviar!

You do not have to be a cook trained by a French chef to make this delicious dish. Do not go by the scary French name. It is just chicken liver with creamy cheese.

You make the Chilled Crème with **1 teaspoon unflavored gelatin, 3 tablespoons water, 2 packages of 3 ounces each of cream cheese, cut into chunks, 13 ounces can of consommé, chilled and one tablespoonful of Madeira.**

The pâté is going to be made up of **one cup of butter, divided into 2, one onion, peeled and quartered, 1 teaspoon dry mustard, half a teaspoonful of salt, ¼ teaspoon each of curry powder, cloves and ground pepper, and a dash of cayenne. You also need 1 pound of chicken livers, 1 teaspoon unflavored gelatin, 3 tablespoons water, half a cup of whipping cream and 2 tablespoons full of Madeira. Cognac is also going to do here.**

Making the Chilled Crème –

Sprinkle the gelatin over the water in a small saucepan

Heat the gelatin over low heat until it dissolves. Allow to cool.

Add the dissolved and cooled gelatin, cream cheese, consommé and Madeira to your blender and blend until smooth.

Butter an 8 inch round cake pan. Line it with waxed paper and butter the paper.

Pour in the cheese, consommé mixture. Cover it with plastic wrap and chill until it is firm.

While the chilled crème is chilling, prepare the **pâté**

Melt half of the butter in a skillet or a saucepan.

Add the onions, dry mustard, curry, salt, cloves, cayenne and pepper. Cook and stir over medium heat until the onion is tender.

Add the chicken liver and cook and stir until they are no longer pink in color. Do not over cook, otherwise they might lose their juiciness and get over tough.

Turn the chicken liver mixture into your processor and blend until smooth.

Sprinkle the gelatin over the water in a small saucepan. Heat it over to the heat until it dissolves. Allow to cool.

Add the Cognac, cream, and the remaining half cup butter, cut in chunks to the liver in the processor.

Add the cooled gelatin to the liver mixture in the processor and blend again until smooth.

Remove the plastic wrap from the chilled crème in the pan and pour the chicken liver mixture over it.

Covered the pâté with a plastic wrap and chill for several hours.

To serve on covered the pâté and invited up on a serving platter. Garnish it with green pepper and tomato or capsicum, if desired.

Makes 25 to 30 appetizer servings.

Appetizers are normally served with cocktails. That is why they have to have an assertive flavor. That is why cheese dishes are so good as appetizers.

Quiches (pronounced keesh, rhyming with Sheesh!), especially those with Roquefort cheese fit the bill adequately here. They are going to work very well with martinis.

This quiche is going to combine a strong cheese flavor, with a velvet smooth texture. You can either serve it hot or cold. The filling is, of course going to be made with the help of your food processor/blender.

Quiche au Roquefort

Pronounced Keesh -Oh- RohK-4.

Bake a pastry shell using the instructions given in the appendix and after you have made the pastry shell with the help of a blender.

To make the quiche. You need a 9 inch pastry shell, 1 cup light cream or half and half, 4 ounces of cream cheese, 4 ounces of Roquefort cheese, 3 eggs, 4 green onions, chopped in short lengths, 1/4 teaspoon salt and white pepper.

After you have baked the pastry shell in a 375°F oven, you will need to put in the filling. Bake it in a 375°F oven for 5 minutes in a pie pan or a flan dish.

While the pastry shell is baking, blend the cream cheese, Roquefort, cream and eggs until it is smooth. Add the onions and the seasonings and blend until the onions are chopped.

Pour the filling into a partially baked pie shell and return it into the oven for 30 – 35 minutes or until a knife inserted near the center comes out clean.

Cool the quiche for 5 – 10 minutes before cutting it into thin wedges. You can serve it warm or chilled.

This is going to make 18 appetizer servings.

For a 9 ½ inch flan dish, you can use the following amounts – 1 ¾ cup light cream or half and half, 8 ounces of cream cheese, 6 ounces of Roquefort cheese and 5 eggs.

Pastry Shell

In many parts of the East, we have a food processor accessory which kneads the dough for us. That is because making fresh dough for baking the bread every day is a part of our traditional cuisine. So naturally, local manufacturers decided that you just needed to add the flour, water and press the button and there you were, you had beautifully kneaded dough in less than 30 seconds.

So any house maker buying a new machine is immediately going to ask – does this food processor have an *atta kneader*. If the shopkeeper says no, she is going to look for a food processor, who gives her this function either inbuilt in the machine or as an accessory.

So if you have one of these accessories, you can make amazingly soft and rich pastry dough for pastry shells, pies and tarts.

2 cups all-purpose flour, half a teaspoonful of salt, half a cup of very cold or frozen butter, 1/4 cup of ice water

Measure the flour and the salt into the processor. Add the butter chunks and mix by turning the motor on and off in short bursts, until the mixture is of the consistency of coarse meal.

With the motor running, pour the ice water in through the feed tube and mix until the dough forms a ball. If the dough seems too soft, add a tablespoon or so more of the flour and mix until it is incorporated.[2]

Roll out the dough to the desired size and thickness on a lightly floured surface. Refrigerate any leftovers out to use for tarts and other pastries. This is going to make enough of pastry for a double crust, 9 inch pie. That is done by rolling out the dough to a circle about 2 inches larger in diameter than the pie plate or flan dish to be used.

Tip – if you are baking the pastry shell, bake it for 4 minutes. To prevent the pastry from puffing, line the raw shell with waxed paper and top the paper with

---

[2] . You can also make this dough by using a blender. Combine the flour and the butter in the blender container, and then mix the water in by hand.

peas, rice, or dry beans. While the shell bakes, you can assemble all the ingredients for the quiche filling.

Learn how to bake the pastry shell in the Appendix.

Cheese Wafers

These are tender and cookie like. They are delicious with a glass of wine, with fruit, with salad or just when you are feeling like a cheese snack. They are definitely addictive. Use a shredding blade to shred the cheese.

8 ounces of chilled cheddar cheese or any other aged cheese.
3 cups all-purpose flour
One teaspoonful salt
1 cup butter
4 ounces walnuts

Shred the cheese and put aside. Now put the salt, flour and butter in the food processor – blender blade or container. Blend until crumbly.

Add the cheese and the nuts into this mixture. Mix just until the nuts are chopped coarsely.

Turn the dough out onto waxed paper and make it into a ball.

Divide the dough into half and form each into a roll about 2 inches in diameter.

Wrap these rolls up in protective wrap and chill for several hours.

Slice each cheese wafer 1/8 inches thick and arrange them on lightly greased baking sheets.

Bake them in a pre-heated 35°F oven for about 10 to 12 minutes or until they are browned lightly.

You are going to get up to 5 dozen wafers.

You can use different variations like adding the herbs and spices of your choice before blending the salt, butter and flour. Try 1 teaspoon of caraway seeds, half a teaspoonful of bishops weed, or dill, one – 2 teaspoons poppy seeds. I cannot do without a hefty and hearty sprinkling of freshly roasted cumin seeds, some pepper and of course Bishops Weed.

Ham and Cheese Snacks

Cheeses are excellent as snacks

If you find yourself inundated with surprise guests, you can make this hearty appetizer in next to no time.

One can deviled ham – 4 ½ ounces, half a small onion, peeled, 3 sprigs parsley, 2 tablespoons full of butter, softened, half a teaspoonful of prepared mustard, 8 slices of toasted white bread and 8 slices of cheddar cheese.

In the food processor or in your blender, combine the deviled ham, onion, parsley, butter, and mustard. Blend until the onion and the parsley are finely chopped.

Spread the ham mixture on the toast slices.Top each toast slice with a cheese slice.

Broil/grill several inches from heat for about 3 minutes or until cheese starts to melt. Cut the slices into half and serve.

16 snacks for all your hungry guests. Keep 'em delicious appetizers coming.[3]

---

[3] I added one teaspoonful of Worcestershire sauce to this deviled ham mixture and added to the zest and zing quotient. The only problem is that even though I have given this recipe to all of my guests – they demanded it – they say it does not taste the same as when I make it. Talk about getting somebody else to do the work for you, especially when you appreciate her snacks!

Crunchy Garden Vegetable Dip

This is a fast to make good to eat Tangy flavored garden dip, which you can use as a perfect appetizer for vegetables.

Just put these items in a blender and mix to get one and a half cups

One onion, chopped, 1 cup cottage cheese, one package cream cheese in chunks – 3 ounces – 1 tablespoon lemon juice, 1 teaspoon prepared horseradish, 1 teaspoon celery salt, ¼ teaspoon dried mustard, one vegetable bouillon cube crushed or one packet vegetable broth base.

Put all these items in the blender and mix till smooth.

Salmon Savory

If you are calorie conscious, you can serve chilled on lettuce leaves with raw vegetable pieces. Works very well with whiskey/Bourbon. You can also use yogurt instead of the sour cream.

16 ounces can of salmon, drained, 1 cup sour cream/yogurt, one green onion, 2 tablespoons lemon juice, half a teaspoon dried dill weed, half a teaspoon salt, one loaf of bread slices or lettuce leaves, or raw vegetables slices

Combine the salmon, cream, onion, lemon juice, dill, and salt in the food processor. Grind until the onions are chopped.

Place about 1 tablespoon full of the mixture on each bread slice. Place the slices on an ungreased baking sheet. Bake in a preheated 400°F oven for 10 to 15 minutes or grill until the mixture dries.

Serve cold, by covering the salmon and chilling for a number of hours to blend the flavors. Serve it on a bed of lettuce and raw vegetables. This can be used as a dip or you can use this recipe to make 32 tasty appetizers.

Soups

Soup of the evening, beautiful soup. Soups are not only nourishing and filling, but you can make them really quickly by either cooking them or making them traditionally by mixing up ingredients by hand and serving.

Gazpacho Soup

This is a traditional Spanish soup, which you can easily call fire and ice. That is because it is eaten cold, but it is hot because of the amount of chilies added to it.

You can control the amount of fire by varying the Cayenne or just adding hot pepper sauce

The contrasting texture of coarsely chopped vegetables and croutons can also be added before serving cold.

Chilled, this soup is delicious, but you can also have all the ingredients chilled ahead of time to shorten the refrigeration time, after you have made it.

2 medium tomatoes, peeled and quartered, one onion, chopped, one green pepper quartered and seeded, one cucumber, cut in chunks, 2 cups Tomato juice, 1 tablespoon tarragon or wine vinegar, half – 1 teaspoons salt, cayenne pepper and/or hot pepper sauce to taste.

Garnish with one cucumber, cut in chunks, one green pepper quartered and seeded, one tomato, one onion, peeled and quartered, one stalk celery, 2 tablespoons oil, one clove of garlic, crushed and minced, 2 slices of bread, cubed.

Soup – put the tomatoes, onion, green pepper and cucumber into the processor. Blend until smooth. Pour the soup into a container for refrigeration.

Add the tomato juice, vinegar and reasoning. Mix well. Chill thoroughly.

Garnish before serving, with the cucumber, green pepper, tomato, onion and celery, chopped coarsely. This can be done by putting one vegetable at a time into the processor or blender container and turning the machine on and off, in short bursts.

Covered the chopped vegetables and chill while preparing the croutons.

Heat the oil in the skillet, add the garlic and cook briefly.

Add the cubes of bread. Cook and stir over medium heat until they are browned. Remove the croutons from the skillet and drain on paper towels.

To serve, ladle the smooth vegetable mixture into chilled bowls. Sprinkle with the chopped vegetables and top with croutons.

Makes 6 servings.

Vichyssoise Cresson

Pronounced veeshee so ahsse kreh song.

This is the classic potato leek soup. You are going to give a new flavor and color to this soup by adding something interesting – watercress. This is an immensely nourishing cold and satisfying soup.

The chopping of all the ingredients is going to be done in your blender.

3 medium-sized leeks/6 to 8 green onions washed and cut into small pieces, ¼ cup butter, 4 medium potatoes, peel and cut in chunks, 1 quart chicken stock, one bunch watercress, 1 teaspoon salt, – white pepper, 1 cup whipping cream, watercress for garnishing

Chop the leeks in the food processor or blender. Melt the butter in a large saucepan. Add the leeks and cook until they are limp – about 5 minutes.

Chop the potatoes in the food processor or blender, by turning the motor on and off in short bursts.

Add the potatoes to the leeks, along with the stock. Cover and simmer for about 15 minutes or until very tender.

Pour the potato mixture into the processor or blender and blend until very smooth.

Add the watercress and seasonings and blend until finely chopped.

For the mixture into a large container, stir in the cream, cover and chill thoroughly. Garnish with watercress. Makes 8 servings.

Minestrone

This is an extremely popular Italian soup and rather expensive when you eat it in Italian restaurants. But make it at home often, and enjoy all the compliments, thanks to your food processor.

The fresher the vegetables are, the tastier the minestrone is going to be. Use your slicing blade or your multipurpose blade to chop all these items in a jiffy.

1 cup dried navy beans, 2 large onions, peeled and quartered, 2 tablespoons olive oil, 4 medium carrots, peeled, 2 medium potatoes, peeled and cut into chunks, one small head cabbage, quartered and cut into wedges, 2 stalks of celery, cut in short lengths, two medium zucchini, 1 quart chicken broth

stock or bouillon 8 – 10, red tomatoes, one teaspoonful salt, 1 cup your favorite pasta.

Cover the beans with water in a large saucepan. Heat until just boiling. Then remove the pan from the heat, cover and let it stand, for one hour.

Meanwhile, slice the onions and sauté them in the oil until tender. Slice the carrots and the potatoes set them aside. Slice the cabbage, celery, and the zucchini and set them aside in a separate bowl.

Add the chicken broth, the beans along with the potatoes and carrots. Cover and simmer for about 30 minutes or until the vegetables are almost tender.

Stir in the tomatoes, sautéed onions, cabbage, celery, zucchini, salt and pasta. Simmer, uncovered, 15 – 30 minutes or until the vegetables are tender. Makes 8 – 10 generous servings.

Chowder

If you are living in a place near the sea and have access to plenty of seafood, how come you have not tried out seafood chowder? This dish is flavorful, hearty and satisfying – everything you should expect from a seafood chowder. About 150 years ago, it would have taken a lot of time to make this dish, especially with all the chopping involved, but with a multi-food processor, all this is done in the fraction of the time.

So here is the traditional chowder recipe modified for the 21st century.

For this you need **one and a half cups of small shelled macaroni, one medium onion, peeled and quartered, 2 stalks of celery, cut into small lengths, 1 clove of garlic, ¼ cup of butter, 1/3 cup of dry white wine, 1 teaspoon chicken base, 1 teaspoon salt. The herbs which are going to use include half a teaspoon each of thyme, nutmeg and pepper and one bay leaf**

Then collect 5 tablespoons full of flour, half a cup of cold water, 1 pound of codfish fillets fresh or frozen – thaw beforehand if frozen, and cube – 6 oysters fresh, or one can 10 ounces of frozen oysters, drained. Reserve the liquid, half a medium green pepper, seeded, one can – 8 ounces of evaporated milk, one can, 8 ounces of minced clams – drained, reserve

liquid, one can 4 ounces of tiny shrimp, drained, reserve liquid, 2 or 3 sprigs of parsley, 2 ounce jar of pimiento, drained.

Cook the macaroni – macaroni shells are best – in boiling salted water, 2 quarts water +1 tablespoon salt until tender – about 8 minutes. Drain.

Chop the onion, celery and garlic medium fine in the food processor.

Melt the butter in the large saucepan. Add the chopped vegetables and sauté for 5 minutes.

Combine the reserve liquid from the clams, shrimp and oysters and add just enough of water to measure 3 cups. Add this liquid to the sautéed mixture.

Stir in the wine, chicken base and seasonings. Cover and simmer for 15 minutes.

Blend the flour and cold water to a smooth paste. Add it to the liquid in the pan, stirring constantly. Cook and stir until smooth and thickened.

Now add the codfish and the oysters.

Chop the green pepper, medium fine. Add it to the pan. Simmer uncovered for 10 to 15 minutes.

Remove the bay leaf, then stir in the macaroni shells, milk, clams and shrimp.

Chop the parsley and add it to the chowder. Chop the pimiento and add it.

Heat to simmering and serve for 8 – 10 hearty servings.

Oriental Spinach Soup

This is an unusual broth, which can be the ideal accompaniment to any sort of exotic oriental meal. Use a blender or a steel blade of your processor and a slicing blade to prepare it.

4 chicken breasts, 4 cups of water, half a pound of fresh mushrooms, 1 pound fresh spinach, 2 green onions, chopped up in short lengths, half a cup of soy sauce

Cook the chicken in the water in the saucepan until tender.

Meanwhile, cut the ends of the stems of the mushrooms and slice them with the slicing blade. Set them aside.

Rinse the spinach in lukewarm water. Remove the stems and drain. Chop the spinach in small amounts at a time in the food processor. Set aside.

Reserve the broth and drain the chicken. Skin and bone it and then cut it up into 1 inch cubes. Chop the chicken with the onions – a small amount at a time in the food processor or blender container.

Combine the chicken and the onions, reserve mushrooms, spinach, reserved broth and soy sauce in a saucepan. Bring the soup to a boil. Reduce the heat and simmer for 5 minutes.

Makes 6 – 8 servings.

Quick Soup Ideas

Soup Base for Cream Soups

If you are looking for quick soup ideas, the basic recipe for cream soups is obtained by measuring 2 tablespoons full of butter in a saucepan, adding 2 tablespoons full of flour and cooking and stirring, until bubbly.

Then add 1 cup of milk and salt and pepper to taste, to make **the soup base.**

Then you can make your own improvisations.

You can chop an onion in the food processor and sauté it in the butter before adding the flour, if you wish.

You can also purée almost any cooked vegetable starting from asparagus to zucchini. You can also shred 4 ounces of cheese and stir in the soup base for an instant cheese soup.

Traditional cabbage soup can be made by slicing some cabbage, then cooking in chicken stock or broth or beef bouillon until it is crisply – tender. Shred some cheese to sprinkle over the top, just before serving.

Salads

Waldorf Salad

It is said that this salad was invented by a chef in the Waldorf in the early 20s – 30s, using tart apples, crunchy nuts and celery to make a winning combination. The apples can be sliced with the slicing blade when chopping the nuts and celery, done to the blender or use your steel blade.

3 Crisp apples, peeled, 1 tablespoon almond juice, 1 cup walnuts, 3 stalks of celery, chopped in small lengths, half a cup of mayonnaise, half a cup of sour cream, 2 teaspoons sugar, ¼ cups raisins, crisp salad greens.

Half the apples and remove seeds and core. Slice the apples with the slicing blade and transfer to a bowl. Toss with the lemon juice so that they do not lose their color.

Chop the nuts using the steel blade of your processor. Add the nuts to the bowl with the apples. Chop the celery and add it to the apples.

Stir together the mayonnaise, sour cream and sugar, then add them along with the raisins to the apple mixture.

Chill at least one hour to blend all the flavors. Serve the salads on crisp salad greens, like lettuce.

Marinated Fresh Vegetables

Any vegetable can be used to make marinated vegetables

These vegetables are full of color, flavor and crunch and you can prepare them well ahead of time. Leftovers are also going to keep beautifully.

3 stalks celery, 4 large carrots, 3 green peppers, seeded, 3 small onions, peeled, and 3 tomatoes.

Use your food processor's slicer attachment to slice all these vegetables one after another. Start with the carrots. After you have cut off the stem ends and the tips, slice and add them to a bowl. Do this to the celery, green peppers and the onions and also with the tomatoes.

After that pour Basil French dressing over the vegetables. Gently toss the salad to mix or leave the vegetables in these layers. Cover and refrigerate overnight.

Salad Dressings

Basil French Dressing

Apart from basil, you can also use any herbs available to you to make this French dressing.

You can use this simple dressing to add spice to salads, makes greens, and even apples and citrus fruit.

¼ cup tomato sauce, 1/3 cup red wine vinegar, 1 cup of salad oil, 1 tablespoon sugar, 1 teaspoons salt, 1 teaspoon basil, 1 teaspoon Worcestershire sauce, ¼ teaspoon dry mustard, a little bit of pepper, 1/8 teaspoon hot pepper sauce, one clove of garlic

Combine all the ingredients together in the processor and blend until they are smooth. Chill in a covered container until ready to use. You are going to get one 2/3 cups of dressing.

This was considered to be the trickiest of all cooking techniques once upon a time. That was because you had to trickle the oil drop by drop into the egg mixture. But thanks to a food processor, you are going to get foolproof mayonnaise, all the time.

Homemade mayonnaise has a flavor that surpasses anything bought in the store. Of course, it is perfect for sandwiches, spring salads, fruit salads, or as a base for other salad dressings.

You make it with **1 cup salad oil, 2 eggs, 2 tablespoons lemon juice or vinegar, 1 teaspoon sugar, 1 teaspoon dried mustard, half a teaspoon salt and a dash of cayenne pepper.**

All right, let me confess. I cannot resist adding a clove of garlic and some of my own preferred herbs including onions and other spices to my version of mayonnaise. But the basic ingredients are given above.

Pour ¼ cups of the oil into the processor – using the blender container – and add the eggs, lemon juice, sugar, mustard, salt and cayenne.

A French friend told me that mayonnaise could only be made with the white of an egg with absolutely no yellow in it. I have been making it with complete eggs and could not care less about whites and yellows! The end result is equally tasty.

Proceed for about 5 to 10 seconds on high speed.

Now remove the pusher from the feed tube of your processor, if you have it. You will need to trickle filing a constant and thin stream, through the feed tube with the motor still running. Process until all the oil is added and the mayonnaise is thick and smooth.

Transfer the mayonnaise to a covered container for refrigerator storage. Mayonnaise should be thick and smooth. We are going to get 1 2/3 cups of salad dressing.

When you have made mayonnaise, this can be used as a base to make a traditional green goddess dressing.

Green Goddess Dressing

This is a simple and ordinary mayonnaise with more herbs and spices. Like I said I could not resist **cloves of garlic and onions in my mayonnaise. So, take 1 ¼ cups of mayonnaise, 4 sprigs of parsley, 2 green onions, 2 tablespoons full of lemon juice or wine vinegar or tarragon vinegar, one clove of garlic, half a teaspoonful of salt, dash of pepper and half a cup of sour cream.**

Pour the mayonnaise in your blender, add the parsley, onions, lemon juice or vinegar, garlic and blend just until the onions are finely chopped.

Add the sour cream and blend just until mixed.

Transfer the dressing into a covered container for refrigerator storage.

Makes about 2 ½ cups of dressing.

Main Dishes

Old Chinatown burger

Craving a burger? Consider this to be a robust junk food sandwich, especially when you are adding oriental flavor to make up a luncheon or a snack. You can also use this for a family supper Main dish.

2 slices firm white bread chunks, 4 green onions, half a medium green pepper, seeded, one can of water chestnuts – 6 ½ ounces, and drained, 1 pound of pork sausage, one egg, 2 tablespoons dry Sherry, 2 tablespoons soya bean sauce, one small clove of garlic, ¼ teaspoon ground ginger, 6 large and rich sesame seeds Hamburger buns, butter, 1 cup bean sprouts, rinsed and well-drained, sweet and sour sauce

Put the bread into the food processor or the blender and make bread crumbs. Pour the crumbs into a large bowl.

Finely chop the green onions and add them to the breadcrumbs.

Finely chop the green pepper and water chestnuts and add them to the above mixture.

Add the sausage, egg, sherry, soy sauce, garlic and ginger and mix well. Chill the mixture several hours for easier handling, if you wish.

When you are ready to cook it, ship the burger mixture into 6 patties and grill until they are done. You can toast the buns after splitting, butter them, and use the burgers to make your hamburgers.

Divide the bean sprouts on the bottom half of the buns and top each with the Patty.

Spoon equal amounts of sweet and sour sauce over each patty. Close the sandwiches with the top of the bun.

Sweet and Sour Sauce

Pineapples make an excellent sweet and sour sauce.

Half a cup of crushed pineapple, drained, half a cup of ketchup, 2 tablespoons vinegar, 2 tablespoons orange marmalade, 1 tablespoon prepared mustard.

Combine all the ingredients in a small saucepan, heat the mixture until the marmalade melts. Makes 1 cup sweet and sour sauce to be used on 6 burgers, sandwiches.

I could not resist adding lettuce leaves, tomatoes and pieces of ham to these giant burgers. If I am eating what is considered to be junk food, let me add something which I like and which is really healthy!

Ham Loaf

Ham leftovers can be used to make a ham loaf

Nothing can be better than this old-fashioned ham loaf for a robust and satisfying main dish. You can use ham leftovers to make this ham loaf after you have cooked and served a ham.

1 pound of smoked cooked ham, cubed, 1 pound lean boneless pork, cubed, one medium onion, peeled and halved 3 slices rye bread, torn into pieces, 4 sweet pickles, one egg.

Place all the ingredients in the food processor and mix until the meat is finely chop and all the ingredients are thoroughly combined.

Or you can grind all the ingredients in the grinder, and then mix them well by hand or with your mixer.

Pack the mixture in an 8.5 x 4.5" loaf pan and bake it in a preheated oven at 350°F for about 1 ¼ hours.

Makes 6 – 8 servings.

Quick Main Dish Ideas

Make a basic quiche mixture of 1 ½ cups light cream, 4 eggs, – 4 ounces of shredded cheese, and then add anything else you like. You can also chop a cup of leftover cooked meat and vegetables, cook and crumble bacon, brown and crumble ground beef and sausages and shred some carrots. Pour into a 9 inch pie shell and bake. Makes 6 servings.

If you just have some cooked poultry left over, you can make it into a super sandwich spread. Finely chop enough of me to make about 1 cup and then blend it, along with half a cup of mayonnaise, a little bit of celery or green pepper, some salts, nuts and pepper to taste. Has to go, good to eat. We are going to get one and a half cups

Pizza

Pizza made my style is going to have a chewy crust, and a savory topping. You will be amazed at how quickly you can make dough in the food processor as instructed above.

For this you need **one package active dry yeast, 2/3 cups warm water, 2 cups all-purpose flour, half a teaspoonful of salt, 2 tablespoons oil, 12 ounces of mozzarella cheese, chilled, one small onion, peeled and quartered, half a pound of mushrooms, 2 tablespoons butter, half –/3 cups tomato sauce,oregano,thyme, garlic salt to taste and anchovies, if you can get them.**

Dissolve the yeast in water in a small bowl.

Combine the flour and the salt in the food processor or mixing bowl.

Add the yeast and the oil. Blend until smooth and the dough begins to form a ball and leaves the side of the bowl of the container.

Turn the dough out on a greased bowl. Turn the dough to grease the top. Cover it and let it rise in a warm place for about 2 hours, or until it is doubled in bulk.

Pat and stretch the dough to fit into a 12 inches pizza pan.

Shred the cheese and set it aside. Slice the onions and the mushrooms. Melt the butter in a skillet. Add the onion and the mushrooms and sauté until tender.

Sprinkle the tomato sauce over the dough. Sprinkle with the cheese, onion, mushrooms, herbs and garlic salt and anchovies, if desired.

Bake in a preheated 400°F oven for 25 minutes.

This completed pizza is going to give you one 12 inch pizza.

It can be frozen up to one week before baking.

Welsh Rarebit

How do you get velvet smooth rarebit? That is done by stirring the beer and the cheese constantly over low heat until they are thoroughly blended.

This is an excellent light supper, which you can also serve with English muffins that sliced fresh tomatoes.

8 ounces of chilled cheddar cheese or any other sharp tasting cheese, half a cup of beer, 1 teaspoon of Worcestershire sauce, a little bit of paprika, a little bit of pepper, one egg, 2, tomatoes, 4 English muffins split and toasted

Shred the cheese with your shredding blade. Place the cheese and beer in a saucepan. Warm it over low heat until the cheese melts. Stir it constantly, until the mixture becomes smooth and begins to thicken.

Add the Worcestershire sauce, paprika and pepper.

Stir in the egg yolk. Cook over low heat until thickened and smooth – over 5 minutes.

Chop the tomatoes into small pieces and stir them into the cheese mixture. To serve, spoon the sauce over the English muffins – you get 4 servings.

Desserts

2 Tone Brownies

You can sprinkle chocolate sauce over these brownies

This is for all those people who cannot resist chocolate. These Brownies have a white ripple of cream cheese.

For 18 Brownies, you need 1 cup butter, cut in chunks, 2 cups +3 tablespoons sugar, 4 eggs, half a teaspoonful of salt, 1 cup of cocoa, 1 ½ to 2 cups walnuts, 1 cup all purpose flour

The filling is going to be made with one 8 hours package of cream cheese, half a cup of sugar, one egg, and half a teaspoonful of vanilla.

Blend the butter, the sugar, the eggs and the salt in the food processor until light and fluffy.

Add the cocoa and the nuts and blend just until the nuts are coarsely chopped

Add the flour and mix just until moistened. Pour half of the batter into a greased 9 x 13 x 2 inch pan. Spoon out the remaining batter and set it aside.

Wash the food processor before making the cream cheese filling.

Put the cream cheese, the sugar, the egg and the vanilla into the food processor and beat until smooth.

Spread the cream cheese mixture over the batter in the pan.

Spread the remaining chocolate batter over the cream cheese. Mix lightly with a spoon or a spatula.

Bake these Brownies in a preheated 350°F oven for 35 to 40 minutes.

Sauces

Hollandaise Sauce

Just like mayonnaise, making Hollandaise sauce has become almost foolproof with the help of a food processor. Just put all these items in your blender and blend.

3 egg yolks, 2 tablespoons lemon juice, half a teaspoonful of salt, sprinkling of paprika and cayenne pepper, half a cup of butter

Put all the ingredients except the butter into the food processor and blend.

Melt the butter just until it liquefies then begins to bubble.

Gradually add the butter to the processor to blend. While the motor is still running. You can do that by opening the top or pouring the butter through the feed tube mixing until smooth and thickened.

Serve the sauce at once. Any leftover sauce should become void and refrigerated. Reheat the sauce over boiling water or by stirring in a very small amount of hot water.

Makes about ¾ cups.

Tomato Sauce

Ripe tomatoes for tomato sauce…

If you have a rich harvest of tomatoes, make this delicious sauce and bottle. You can then try it over pasta, cheese sandwiches, and even beef patties.

One medium carrot, 2 medium onions one stalk of celery, one clove of garlic, half a cup of butter, 3 tablespoons full of flour, 1 can – 10 ½ ounces of beef bouillon, 2 pounds right tomatoes, stemmed and quartered, 2 or 3 sprigs of us, me, half a teaspoonful of sugar, ¼ teaspoonful each of thyme and marjoram and one bay leaf.

Chop the carrot, onion, celery and garlic in a food processor or blender.

Melt the butter in a large saucepan. Add the chopped vegetables and sauté over medium heat 5 to 10 minutes. Do not brown.

Blend in the flour and cook until bubbly.

Add the bouillon and cook and stir until the mixture comes to a boil and is smooth and thick.

Chop the tomatoes in the food processor or blender and add them to the saucepan.

Chop the parsley and add it to the pan along with the sugar and seasoning.

Simmer very slowly for up to 2 hours, stirring occasionally until the sauce is thick.

Strain. If you are not using the sauce at once, cover it lightly and refrigerate or freeze.

Makes about 2 ½ cups.

Appendix

Check out more grandma series books here on Amazon.

Grandma's Books on Amazon

Baking the Pastry Shell

Roll out the pastry, keeping it circular in shape for 2 inches larger than your flan ring or dish.

If you are using a flan ring, place it on the baking sheet. Roll the pastry loosely around the rolling pin and lift it over the rink or the dish to be lined and unroll carefully.

Press the pastry to the shape of the ring, pressing out all air spaces between the ring and the baking sheet or dish as these are going to cause your pastry to bulge.

Trim off the excess pastry by running the rolling pin over the edge of the flan ring. When you are lining a dish, cut away the excess pastry with a knife against the edge of the dish. Prick the base well with a fork.

Baking Your Pastry – Blind Baking

This is the term that is used when a recipe calls for a pastry case to be baked without any filling.

After aligning the pie plate or the slandering with pastry, prick the base well so that there is no air trapped which is going to cause the base to rise.

Line the pastry case with foil. Remember that when you are using foil lining, as long as the pastry base has been well pricked, there is no need to use baking beans. However, the foil has to be crumpled. This foil lining can be kept after you wipe it, and used again.

You can also use grease proof paper. Fill the case with dried beans, macaroni and peas.

These items are known as baking beans. You can return these baking beans to their special jar and use them only for this particular purpose, again and again.

Bake your piecrust till it is done.

You may want to look at this URL about how the professional chefs do the lining of the dish and blind baking!

http://www.youtube.com/watch?v=J4m5iPvzwiA

Conclusion

This book is an introduction to the wonders of the food processors available in the market today. Not only do they give you an opportunity to indulge in all your creative ideas when cooking up brand-new dishes, but they also help in saving you plenty of time by making your kitchen activities, lighter and easier to do.

So before you start cooking, start mixing, grinding, chopping, blending, puréeing and using your food processor as often as you can. You are definitely going to consider this the best kitchen equipment and investment you ever made.

Check out more grandma series books here on Amazon.

Grandma's Books on Amazon

Live Long and Prosper!

Author Bio

Dueep Jyot Singh is a Management and IT Professional who managed to gather Postgraduate qualifications in Management and English and Degrees in Science, French and Education while pursuing different enjoyable career options like being an hospital administrator, IT,SEO and HRD Database Manager/ trainer, movie , radio and TV scriptwriter, theatre artiste and public speaker, lecturer in French, Marketing and Advertising, ex-Editor of Hearts On Fire (now known as Solstice) Books Missouri USA, advice columnist and cartoonist, publisher and Aviation School trainer, ex- moderator on Medico.in, banker, student councilor ,travelogue writer … among other things!

One fine morning, she decided that she had enough of killing herself by Degrees and went back to her first love -- writing. It's more enjoyable! She already has 48 published academic and 14 fiction- in- different- genre books under her belt.

When she is not designing websites or making Graphic design illustrations for clients , she is browsing through old bookshops hunting for treasures, of which she has an enviable collection – including R.L. Stevenson, O.Henry, Dornford Yates, Maurice Walsh, De Maupassant, Victor Hugo, Sapper, C.N. Williamson, "Bartimeus" and the crown of her collection- Dickens "The Old Curiosity Shop," and so on… Just call her "Renaissance Woman") - collecting herbal remedies, acting like Universal Helping Hand/Agony Aunt, or escaping to her dear mountains for a bit of exploring, collecting herbs and plants and trekking.

Our books are available at

1. Amazon.com
2. Barnes and Noble
3. Itunes
4. Kobo
5. Smashwords
6. Google Play Books

Check out some of the other JD-Biz Publishing books

Gardening Series on Amazon

Country Life Books

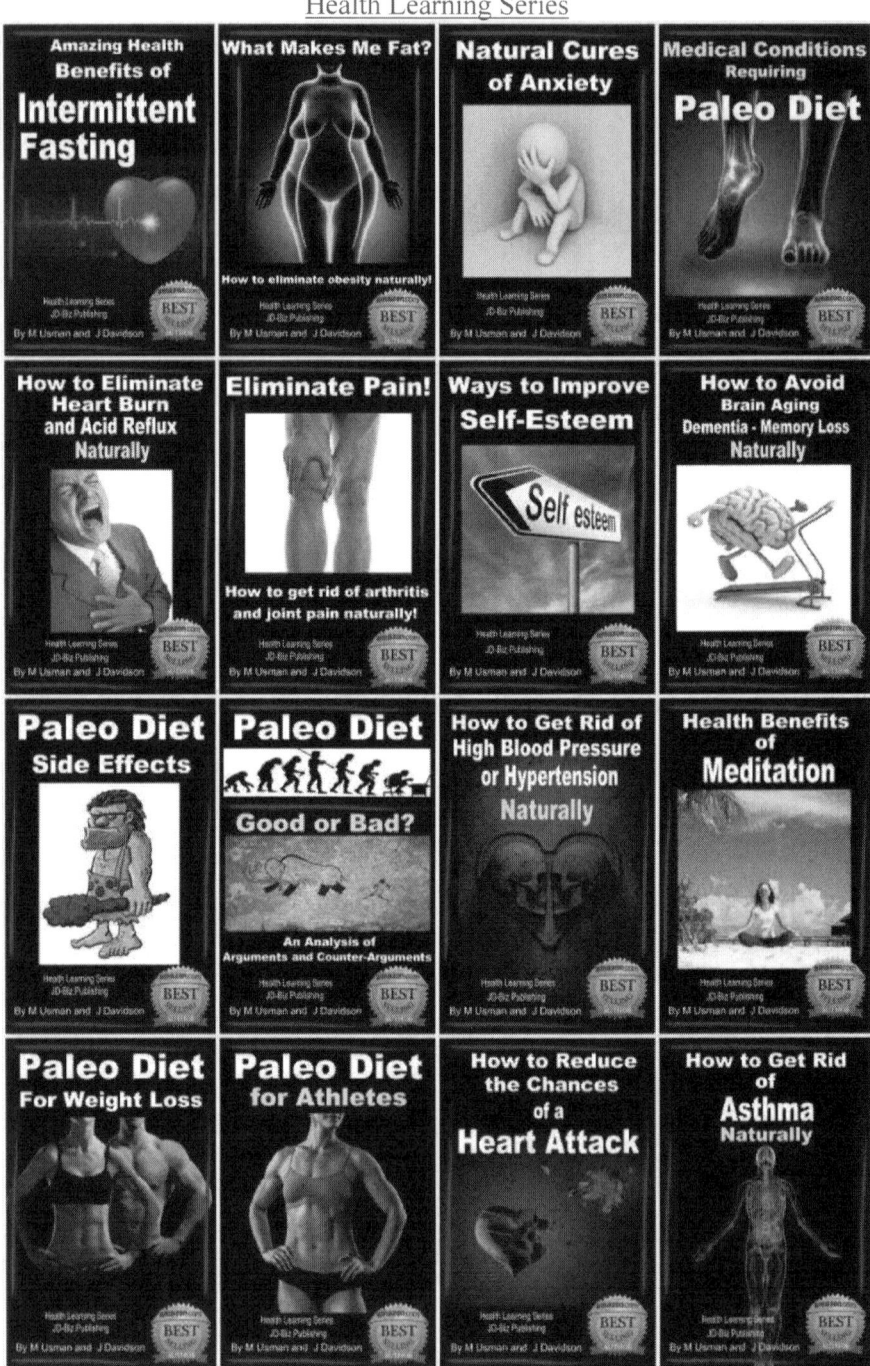

Amazing Animal Book Series

Learn To Draw Series

How to Build and Plan Books

Publisher

JD-Biz Corp

P O Box 374

Mendon, Utah 84325

http://www.jd-biz.com/

Mendon Cottage Books

P O Box 374, Mendon Utah 84325

Printed in Great Britain
by Amazon.co.uk, Ltd.,
Marston Gate.